DESERT WISDOM

DESERT WISDOM

Sayings from the Desert Fathers

YUSHI NOMURA

Doubleday & Company, Inc.
Garden City, New York
1982

Library of Congress Cataloging in Publication Data
Main entry under title:

Desert wisdom.

''[Translated from] texts found in Patrologia Latina,
volume 73, compiled by J.P. Migne, Paris, 1849, and in
Patrologia Graeca, volume 65, compiled by J.P. Migne,
Paris, 1858''—
1. Christian life—Miscellanea.   2. Monastic and
religious life—Miscellanea.   3. Asceticism—Miscellanea.
I. Nomura, Yushi.
BV4495.D47   1982   248.4'7   82-45488
ISBN 0-385-18078-0
Copyright © 1982 by Yushi Nomura
Introduction Copyright © 1982 by Henri J. M. Nouwen
All Rights Reserved
Printed in the United States of America
First Edition

For my father, a son of the Samurai, from whom I inherited
a sense of tradition, and for my late mother, whose way of life
led me to the Christian faith.

AUTHOR'S NOTE

These stories and sayings of the Christian hermits from fourth- and fifth-century Egypt have a unique place in Christian tradition. They have been a source of inspiration to the Western monastic movement throughout its history and are considered by scholars to be one of the important groups of documents among early Christian writings. Yet to others they are not well known today. As an effort to convey their richness and uniqueness to a wider group, I selected and translated these stories from the Latin and Greek texts, and visually interpreted them with Japanese brush and ink.

For this translation I used texts found in *Patrologia Latina,* volume 73, compiled by J. P. Migne, Paris, 1849, and in *Patrologia Graeca,* volume 65, compiled by J. P. Migne, Paris, 1858. I have tried to retain the simple, down-to-earth quality of the texts by translating them into plain modern English and have used gender-inclusive language wherever possible. I believe that the spirit of these stories is inclusive even where the language is not and so have used the drawings themselves to illustrate this. I kept the Aramaic words "Abba" and "Amma" in this translation. They mean "Father" and "Mother" and were widely used to address spiritual fathers and mothers with love and respect.

This project had its beginning in the course on Desert Spirituality and Contemporary Ministry at Yale Divinity School, which was taught by Henri J. M. Nouwen. Yet Henri's understanding and encouragement has far exceeded the classroom. If I had not had such overwhelming support, spiritual and otherwise, from this wonderful teacher and great friend, it would have been utterly impossible for this book to take its present form. Karin Johnson not only helped me to correct and refine my English style, but also painstakingly checked the translation against the original Latin and Greek texts and gave me many important suggestions. Through her loving personality, Karin has given me a sense of assurance in the course of this work. There are numerous people involved, directly and indirectly, in the various stages of this project. Particularly, my dear friends at Yale Divinity School, the soup kitchen in New Haven, and the Church of the Living Hope in East Harlem, New York City, have been my sources of encouragement and inspiration from the beginning. The support and kindness shown by my editor at Doubleday, Patricia Kossmann, and her assistant, Kevin F. Donlon, were far beyond their professional roles. It was their warmth and patience that brought me to the completion of this book. Because of its rather unusual format, that is, calligraphy and Japanese brush painting on rice paper, Doug Bergstreser played an essential role as Art Director. It was his profound understanding and generous technical assistance, combined with his gentle personality, that enabled me to execute the artwork of this book. Finally, I would like to thank my father and sister for their understanding of this project, which kept me far from home.

Yushi Nomura
New Haven, Connecticut
18 April 1982

INTRODUCTION

This is a book with stories from the desert. They are translated, handwritten, and decorated by my friend Yushi Nomura. I am grateful for the opportunity to introduce this splendid book because from the moment the plans for this project were first expressed, I have felt very closely connected with their realization.

In this introduction I want to do three things. First of all, I want to describe the remarkable way in which these desert stories bridged the distance between Japan, the United States, Holland, and Peru and linked me in a very personal way to Yushi and his work. Second, I would like to present the desert fathers and desert mothers and show how their spiritual struggle and ours are essentially the same. Finally, I hope to convince you, who will read these stories, that they have the power to offer not just new insights, but even new life.

I. I am writing these words in Pamplona Alta, a huge barrio at the outskirts of Lima, Peru. Twenty-five years ago this was a raw empty desert. Today this desert has been converted into a city where more than one hundred thousand poor Peruvians try to survive.

I have been here only four weeks, but these four weeks seem ages away from Holland, where I was born, spent an easy youth, became a priest, studied, and taught; ages away, too, from Connecticut in the United States, where I lived and worked with theology students during the last ten years.

What am I doing here in this hot, dusty, desert city? What am I doing in this strange new world with countless little kids running up to me, hugging and kissing me, and using me as a climbing tree; with numerous teenagers playing soccer in the loose yellow sand; with many friendly men and women saying: "Buenos días," "Buenas tardes," or "Buenas noches" and with an occasional drunkard putting his arm around me and raising a profound question about the meaning of life? What am I doing in this treeless place, with loudspeakers shouting local news over the housetops, with squeaking phonographs playing until the early hours of the morning, with thousands of underfed, ugly-looking, barking dogs and even more crowing cocks, with shouting vendors and crying babies, with many curses and tears, and with endless dark fears about the future of it all? Why am I here so far from books, students, discussion groups, and lecture halls? I do not have a precise answer, but I do know that voices from another desert have a lot to do with it. They are the voices of the old Egyptian hermits of the fourth and fifth centuries. Ever since I heard their stories and read their sayings, I knew that there was a wisdom, hidden from the learned and revealed to mere children, worth searching for.

One of these desert fathers was Arsenius, a wealthy, well-educated aristocrat who had left Rome to find his salvation in the desert. Of him the story goes: "One day Abba Arsenius was asking an old Egyptian man for advice about what he was thinking. There was someone who saw this and said to him: 'Abba Arsenius, why is a person like you, who has such a great knowledge of Greek and Latin, asking a peasant like this about your thoughts?' He replied: 'Indeed, I have learned the knowledge of Latin and Greek, yet I have not learned even the alphabet of this peasant.'"

Maybe this is why I am here. To learn a new alphabet from Pablo, Sofía, Pablito, Juanito, and María, the family with whom I live. It is an alphabet that spells patience, humility, joy, hope, and love in a wholly new way: the way of the poor, the way of the victims of oppression and exploitation, the way of the God who became a servant.

While I am finding the desert wisdom in Peru, my friend Yushi Nomura is finding it among the poor in the soup kitchen of New Haven, Connecticut. And to him, too, the Abbas and Ammas from the Egyptian desert are giving answers to his question "Why am I here?" Yushi came from Japan to the United States to study. When he came across the simple but profound stories from the Egyptian desert, his Japanese spirit was so deeply moved that he wanted to write them down in a way that they could be not only read, but also seen and felt. And thus, with his sensitive mind and artistic hand, he drew these ancient words anew so that they would touch more directly the human heart. Yushi knew that letters can do more than convey an idea. The Japanese calligraphers had shown him that carefully drawn letters are themselves a message and can reach deeper into the soul than their meaning alone. Yushi also knew that the Christian monk in Egypt and the Buddhist monk in Japan are no strangers to each other. Both struggle to leave behind the illusions and deceptions of this world and both search for the undying light of God. Therefore Yushi placed the desert stories from Egypt in the monastic milieu of Japan, and so he created a place in which the Buddha and the Christ in him could reach out to each other.

While working in this way, the wisdom of the desert became flesh for him in the poor people of New Haven. In a letter to me in Peru he says: "At the soup kitchen I see more and more jobless people coming by, some taking their children with them. I always love to eat with them, listening to their stories, sharing what I know. They are my friends, teachers, and cheerleaders. And I want to be to them at least as much as they have been to me. When I am talking with them, the Abbas and Ammas from the Egyptian desert come to my heart and tell me what to say. At other times, I see 'Abba and Amma quality' in my friends at the soup kitchen. And that makes me feel as though I were a little brother surrounded by the community of desert fathers and mothers." These wonderful words make me aware how small the distance between Lima and New Haven really is.

Yushi and I met in a classroom of the Yale Divinity School. I spoke about the desert fathers and desert mothers. He listened and took notes. But then it happened that the desert stories started to do their mysterious work of conversion. With his calligraphy and drawings he helped me see more than I had shown him. He became my teacher by making me look at these stories as if I had never seen them before. To us happened what happened in that faraway Egyptian desert many centuries ago: "There was an old man who had a good disciple. One day he was annoyed and drove the disciple out. Yet the disciple sat down outside the cell and waited. When the old man opened the door, he found him sitting there, and repented before him, saying: 'You are my father, for your humility and patience have overcome my narrowmindedness. Come inside! From now on, you are the old man and the father, for sure, and I am the young one and the disciple. For your good works have surpassed my old age.' "

Holland, Peru, Japan, and the United States seem such different worlds, so far apart not only in miles but also in thinking, feeling, and acting. But when Yushi and I came to see our new surroundings through the eyes of the Abbas and Ammas of the desert, we found a unity between us that transcends all distances and all differences, a spiritual unity that cannot be undone by any human-made boundaries.

Thus this book not only contains many stories, but also has its own story, a story of friendship made possible by the divine love reflected to both of us in the wisdom of the desert.

II. Who were these desert fathers and desert mothers? They were men and women who withdrew themselves from the compulsions and manipulations of their power-hungry society in order to fight the demons and to encounter the God of love in the desert. They were people who had become keenly aware that after the period of persecutions and the acceptance of Christianity as a "normal" part of the society, the radical call of Christ to leave father, mother, brother, and sister, to take up the cross and follow him, had been watered down to an acceptable and comfortable religiosity and had lost its converting power. The Abbas and Ammas of the Egyptian desert had left this world of compromise, adaptation, and a lukewarm spirituality and had chosen solitude, silence, and prayer as the new way to be living witnesses of the crucified and risen Lord. Thus they became the new "martyrs," witnessing not with their blood, but with their single-minded dedication to a humble life of manual work, fasting, and prayer.

The life of these ancient hermits can be seen as a hard and often painful struggle to find their true identity. The world they tried to escape is the world in which money, power, fame, success, influence, and good connections are the ways to self-esteem. It is the world that says: "You are what you have." This false identity never gives the security and safety which we are searching for, but throws us in the spiral of a permanent desire for more: more money, more power, more friends, in the illusion that one day we will arrive at that dreamplace where nobody and nothing can harm us. The hermits of the desert were deeply conscious of the fact that not only the society but also the church had been corrupted by this illusion. They escaped into the desert to free themselves from this compulsive self, to shake off the many layers of self-deception and reclaim their true self. In the desert, away from human praise and criticism, they could slowly grow into the knowledge that they are not who people say they are, but who God made them to be: His own sons and daughters, created and recreated in His Spirit. In the desert they came to the realization that as long as they kept trying to find their identity outside of God, they ended up in that vicious spiral of wanting more and more. But there they also discovered that their true identity is securely planted in the first love of God Himself and that this first love frees them from their fearful compulsions and allows them to relate to their own society freely, joyfully, and peacefully.

The way of life of the Abbas and Ammas of the desert makes it clear that finding our true identity is not the simple result of having a new insight. Reclaiming our true self requires a total transformation. It requires a long and often slow process in which we enter more and more into the truth, that is, into a true relationship with God and, through Him, with ourselves.

The desert—the Egyptian desert of the Abbas and Ammas, but also our own spiritual desert—has a double quality: it is wilderness and paradise. It is wilderness, because in the desert we struggle against the "wild beasts" who attack us, the demons of boredom, sadness, anger, and pride. However, it is also paradise, because there we can meet God and taste already His peace and joy. Amma Syncletica said: "In the beginning, there is struggle and a lot of work for those who come near to God. But after that, there is indescribable joy. It is just like building a fire: at first it's smoky and your eyes water, but later you get the desired result. Thus we ought to light the divine fire in ourselves with tears and effort."

It would, however, be a mistake to think that the desert fathers and desert mothers only went to the desert for their own salvation. This was certainly an important aspect of their monastic life, but it was never disconnected from a deep sense of service to the larger Christian community. Their struggle was not just for themselves but also for their fellow Christians. They considered the desert as the place to which the demons withdrew after their destructive work in the cities and towns. They went to the desert to enter into a direct and unambiguous combat with these demons, a combat in the name of the whole church. The hermits of the desert were hermits for others. Thus it is easy to understand that many people from the cities and towns, laypeople, priests, and bishops came to visit them and ask for their advice, for guidance, or just for a word of comfort. It is also quite understandable that they themselves always considered it as their primary obligation to be hospitable to their visitors, and to help the poor and needy. Even the most severe form of asceticism was considered less important than service to the neighbor. That is why one of the wise men of the desert says: "Even if the brother who fasts six days were to hang himself by the nose, he could not equal the one who serves the sick."

Escaping the world was, therefore, for the desert fathers and mothers like escaping from a prison with the intention to liberate the other prisoners too.

III.   From the many desert stories, Yushi Nomura has made a careful selection. The stories he presents in this book are stories that can speak directly to us, who live at least fifteen centuries after they were first written down. They do not require much explanation. What they do require is a spirit of discipleship, that is, a willingness to listen, to learn, and to be converted. They all touch our own spiritual concerns. They respond to our disturbing feelings of anger and our undesirable desires for pleasure and revenge. They point to humility and a nonjudgmental way of life. They compare words with works, speaking with silence, and prayer with thoughts. They offer concrete suggestions about the best way to be a teacher and about how to relate to human rules. They stress the importance of service to the neighbor and they show the fruits of obedience, prayer, and simple trust in God. Undergirding all these concrete hints, suggestions, and counsels is the constant reminder of God's loving and merciful presence in our lives.

During the months in which Yushi was translating these stories from the Greek into the English language, writing them down in beautiful letters and decorating them with Japanese drawings, he wrote me: "These stories have such power that I am able to relate the spirit of the desert to the spirit of the people I meet. These stories have their strength in their short, direct, honest, and simple forms, which came out of the actual life experiences of those brothers and sisters. They are neither legends nor parables, but they are life-giving stories. I am always struck by their power as I stand somewhere between the stories and my friends." This observation, which comes forth from Yushi's own intimate life with these stories, is probably their best introduction, because in these words Yushi captures precisely the reason why we should read them: they are life-giving stories.

The desert fathers and mothers did not offer theories on the spiritual life, they did not give lectures or write essays. They were simple hermits who lived their lives silently, away from the great economic and cultural centers of their day, earning their living with manual work and praying unceasingly. The words we have from them are responses to their fellow hermits, to their disciples, and to their occasional visitors. They are concrete answers to concrete questions. They were never meant to be general truths. They were meant to help a searching brother or sister, to correct an erring fellow monk, to give courage to a despairing friend, or to console a saddened parent.

Paradoxically, however, these sayings which were meant for just one human being have the power to give life to many. They share that power with many Zen and Hasidic sayings. What is most personal, most concrete, and most specific is able to touch the hearts of people living in very different places, in very different times, and in very different circumstances. In their uniqueness they create a large space in which many can find a home. There is realism, humor, irony, reproach, invitation, challenge, and fervent zeal. Together these qualities form the safe and flexible boundaries within which we can move and listen to God's call for us.

One monk who asked his Abba how to live his life received the words: "Rejoice always, pray constantly, and in all circumstances give thanks." Another monk, raising the same question, heard the answer: "Do not be confident in your own righteousness, do not worry about a thing once it's done, and control your tongue and your stomach." And we, who read these divergent responses, smile and realize not only that these two monks must have been quite different, but also that there is space in our own hearts for both of them. Thus the stories from the desert become stories for all of us who seek God with a sincere heart.

To you, who pick up this book and let these sayings enter deeply into your innermost being, Yushi and I want to say that this book is a work of love, the fruit of a deep friendship and a way of whispering into your ears what Abba Bessarion whispered into the ears of Abba Doulas: "God is here, and God is everywhere."

Henri J. M. Nouwen
Peru, 1982

DESERT WISDOM

Abba Poemen said about Abba Pior that every single day he made a fresh beginning.

Abba Isaiah said: When someone wishes to render evil for evil, he is able to hurt his brother's conscience even by a single nod.

Abba Sisoes said: Seek God,
and not where God lives.

One of the fathers said: Just as it is impossible to
see your face in troubled water, so also the soul,
unless it is clear of alien thoughts, is not able
to pray to God in contemplation.

4

It was said about Abba Agathon that for three years he carried a pebble around in his mouth until he learned to be silent.

6

Abba John the Little said: We have abandoned a light burden, namely self-criticism, and taken up a heavy burden, namely self-justification.

Abba John of Thebaid said: Above all things, a
monk ought to be humble. In fact, this is the
first commandment of the Savior who said:
Blessed are the poor in spirit, for theirs is
the kingdom of heaven.

Once the rule was made in Scetis that they should fast for the entire week before Easter. During this week, however, some brothers came from Egypt to see Abba Moses, and he made a modest meal for them. Seeing the smoke, the neighbors said to the priests of the church of that place: Look, Moses has broken the rule and is cooking food at his place. Then the priests said: When he comes out, we will talk to him. When the Sabbath came, the priests, who knew Abba Moses' great way of life, said to him in public: Oh, Abba Moses, you did break the commandment made by people, but you have firmly kept the commandment of God.

Abba Isaiah said to those beginners who were off to a good start, obedient to the tradition of the holy fathers: Take for instance purple cloth: the original dye cannot be removed. And: Just as the young branches can easily be corrected and bent, so can beginners who are obedient.

Abba Mios was asked by a soldier whether God would forgive a sinner. After instructing him at some length, the old man asked him: Tell me, my dear, if your cloak were torn, would you throw it away? Oh, no! he replied, I would mend it and wear it again. The old man said to him: Well, if you care for your cloak, will not God show mercy to his own creature?

11

It was said about John the Little that one day he said
to his older brother: I want to be free from care and
not to work but to worship God without interruption.
And he took his robe off, and went into the desert.
After staying there one week, he returned to his
brother. And when he knocked at the door, his
brother asked without opening it: Who is it?
He replied: It's John, your brother. The brother

said : John has become an angel and is not
among people anymore. Then he begged and said :
It's me! But his brother did not open the door and
left him there in distress until the next morning.
And he finally opened the door and said : If you
are a human being, you have to work again in
order to live. Then John repented, saying :
Forgive me, brother, for I was wrong.

In Scetis, a brother went to see Abba Moses and begged him for a word. And the old man said: Go and sit in your cell, and your cell will teach you everything.

Abba Anthony said: The time is coming when people will be insane, and when they see someone who is not insane, they will attack that person saying: You are insane because you are not like us.

Abba Isaac said : Abba Pambo used to say that the monk's coat should be such that even if he threw it out of the cell and left it for three days, still nobody would take it.

Some old men came to see Abba Poemen, and said to him: Tell us, when we see brothers dozing during the sacred office, should we pinch them so they will stay awake? The old man said to them: Actually, if I saw a brother sleeping, I would put his head on my knees and let him rest.

Abba Evagrius said that there was a brother, called Serapion, who didn't own anything except the Gospel, and this he sold to feed the poor. And he said these words, which are worth remembering: I have even sold the very word which commanded me: Sell everything, and give to the poor.

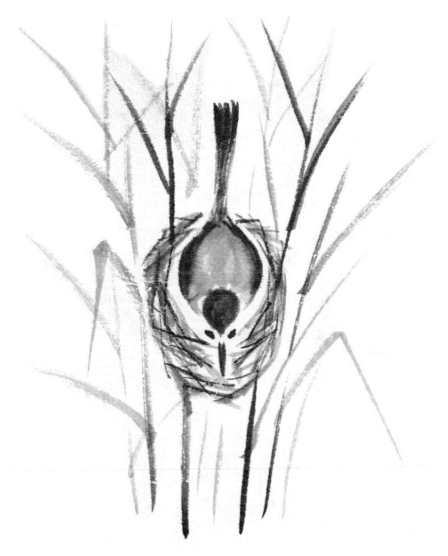

Amma Syncletica said: If you happen to live in a community, do not move to another place, for it will harm you greatly. If a bird leaves her eggs, they never hatch. So also the monk and the nun grow cold and dead in faith by going from place to place.

One day Abba Macarius was on his way back to his cell from the marsh, carrying palm leaves. And look! there was the devil on the road, holding a sickle and trying to attack him. But he couldn't, and said: I am suffering a great deal of violence from you, O Macarius. I do everything you do for sure.

When you fast, I do not eat, and when you keep vigil, I don't go to sleep at all. Yet there is only one thing in which you outdo me. Then Abba Macarius asked: What is it? The devil replied: It is your humility, and because of it I am powerless against you.

21

Abba Silvanus said: Woe to the person whose reputation is greater than his work.

One day Abba Arsenius was asking an old Egyptian man for advice about what he was thinking. There was someone who saw this and said to him: Abba Arsenius, why is a person like you, who has such a great knowledge of Greek and Latin, asking a peasant like this about your thoughts? He replied: Indeed, I have learned the knowledge of Latin and Greek, yet I have not learned even the alphabet of this peasant.

A brother who was living among other brothers
asked Abba Bessarion: What should I do?
The old man replied: Be silent, and do not mea-
sure yourself against the others.

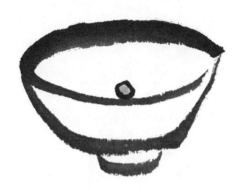

There was a man who was leading an ascetic life and not eating bread. He went to visit an old man. It happened that pilgrims also dropped by, and the old man fixed a modest meal for them. When they sat together to eat, the brother who was fasting picked up a single soaked pea and chewed it. When they arose from the table, the old man took the brother aside and said: Brother, when you go to visit somewhere, do not display your way of life, but if you want to keep to it, stay in your cell and never come out. He accepted what the old man said, and after that behaved like the others whenever he met with them.

Amma Syncletica said: In the beginning, there is struggle and a lot of work for those who come near to God. But after that, there is indescribable joy. It is just like building a fire: at first it's smoky and your eyes water, but later you get the desired result. Thus we ought to light the divine fire in ourselves with tears and effort.

It was said about one brother that when he had woven baskets and put handles on them, he heard a monk next door saying: What shall I do? The trader is coming but I don't have handles to put on my baskets! Then he took the handles off his own baskets and brought them to his neighbor, saying: Look, I have these left over. Why don't you put them on your baskets? And he made his brother's work complete, as there was need, leaving his own unfinished.

A brother came to see Abba Theodore, and started to talk and inquire about things which he himself had not tried yet. The old man said to him ꞉ You have not found a boat, or put your

gear into it, and you haven't even sailed, but you seem to have arrived in the city already! Well, do your work first; then you will come to the point you are talking about now.

It was said about Abba John the Little
that he went away to an old Theban in
Scetis who lived in the desert. Once
his Abba took a piece of dry wood, planted it, and said to him: Water it every
day with a bottle of water until it bears
fruit. The water, however, was so far
away from there that John had to go out
late in the evening and come back the
next morning. Three years later, the
tree came to life and bore fruit.
Then the old man took some of the
fruit and brought it to the church,
and said to the brothers: Take and
eat the fruit of obedience!

An old man said: I never wanted work which was useful to me but loss to my brother. For I have this expectation, that what helps my brother is fruitful for me.

An old man said : Constant prayer quickly straightens out our thoughts.

A brother asked an old man: What shall I do? For many thoughts are bothering me, and I don't know how to fight back. The old man said: Do not fight against all of them, but against one. In fact, all thoughts of monks have a single head - Therefore, you have to figure out which and what kind it is, and fight against it. By doing so, you can defeat the rest of those thoughts.

A brother who had sinned was expelled by the priest from the church. But Abba Bessarion stood up and went out with him, saying: I too am a sinner.

The old men used to say: If you see a young person climbing up to heaven by his own will, hold him by the foot, and pull him down to the ground, for it is just not good for him.

One day, when Abba Agathon was on his way to town to sell small utensils, he saw a leper sitting on the roadside, who asked: Where are you going? Abba Agathon replied: To town, to sell these things. Then he said: Do me a favor, and take me there. So he carried him to the town. Then he said: Put me down wherever you sell those things. So he did. And when he sold one item, the leper asked: How much did you sell it for? So he told him how much it was. Then he said: Buy me something nice. So he bought it. He sold another item.

Then the leper asked = And how much was it? So he told
him the price. Then he said = Buy me this. So he bought
it. After selling everything, he wanted to go. Then the
leper asked = Are you going back? He replied = Sure.
Then he said = Do me a favor again and take me back
to the place where you found me. So he carried him back
to the place where he was. Then he said = You are blessed,
Agathon, by the Lord, in heaven and on earth! As the Abba
lifted his eyes, he saw nobody, for it was an angel of
the Lord who had come to test him.

Abba Hyperichius said: The person who teaches others by actions, not by words, is truly wise.

A brother asked Abba Hieracus: Give me a word. How
can I be saved? The old man said to him: Sit in your cell;
if you are hungry, eat; if you are thirsty, drink; and just
do not speak evil of anyone, and you will be saved.

An old man said: If you have words, but no work, you are like a tree with leaves but no fruit. But just as a tree bearing fruit is also leafy, a person who has good work comes up with good words.

Abba Zeno, the disciple of Abba Silvanus, said:
Never live in a well-known place, nor stay with a
famous person, nor lay a foundation on which
you are going to build a cell someday.

A brother came to visit Abba Sylvanus at Mount Sinai. When he saw the brothers working hard, he said to the old man: Do not work for the food that perishes. For Mary has chosen the good part. Then the old man called his disciple: Zachary, give this brother a book and put him in an empty cell. Now, when it was three o'clock, the brother kept looking out the door, to see whether someone would come to call him for the meal. But nobody called him, so he got up, went to see the old man, and asked: Abba, didn't the brothers eat today? The old

man said: Of course we did. Then he said: Why didn't you call me? The old man replied: You are a spiritual person and do not need that kind of food, but since we are earthly, we want to eat, and that's why we work. Indeed, you have chosen the good part, reading all day long, and not wanting to eat earthly food. When the brother heard this, he repented and said: Forgive me, Abba. Then the old man said to him: Mary certainly needed Martha, and it is really by Martha's help that Mary is praised.

Saint Syncletica said: Just as a treasure exposed
is quickly spent, so also any virtue which becomes
famous or well publicized vanishes. Just as wax
is quickly melted by fire, so the soul is emptied by
praise, and loses firmness of virtue.

Abba Poemen said to Abba Joseph: Tell me how I can become a monk. And he replied: If you want to find rest here and hereafter, say in every occasion, who am I? and do not judge anyone.

Abba John the Little said: No one can build a house from the top down; rather, you build the foundation first and then build upwards. People said to him: What do you mean by that? He said to them: The foundation means your neighbor whom you must win, and you ought to start from there. For all the commandments of Christ depend on this.

An old man said: If you have lost gold or silver, you can find something in place of what you lost. However, if you lose time you cannot replace what you lost.

47

Once a brother committed a sin in Scetis, and the elders assembled and sent for Abba Moses. He, however, did not want to go. Then the priest sent a message to him, saying: Come, everybody is waiting for you. So he finally got up to go. And he took a worn-out basket with holes, filled it with sand, and carried it along.

The people who came to meet him said: What is this,
Father? Then the old man said: My sins are running out
behind me, yet I do not see them. And today I have
come to judge the sins of someone else. When they
heard this, they said nothing to the brother, and pardon-
ed him.

A brother asked Abba Poemen: What does it mean to get angry at one's brother without cause? And he replied: When your brother attacks you, whatever the insults are, if you get angry at him, you are getting angry without cause. Even if he were to pull out your right eye, and to cut off your right hand, if you get angry at him, you are getting angry without cause - Yet if he were to try to take you away from God, then get angry!

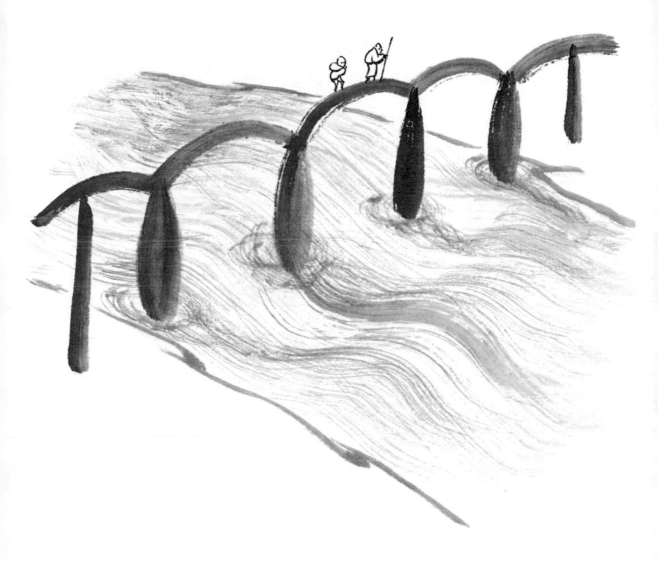

Abba Poemen asked Abba Anthony : What should I do?
The old man said : Do not be confident in your own righteousness, do not worry about a thing once it's done, and
control your tongue and your stomach.

A brother asked Abba Pambo: Why do the spirits hold me back from doing good to my neighbor? The old man said: Do not talk like that, or you will make God a liar. Why don't you say, I don't want to be kind at all? Long ago, God indeed said: I have given you the power to tread upon scorpions and serpents, and over all the strength of the Enemy. Now why don't you stamp down the evil spirit?

A brother who was insulted by another brother came to Abba Sisoes, and said to him: I was hurt by my brother, and I want to avenge myself. The old man tried to console him and said: Don't do that, my child. Rather leave vengeance to God. But he said: I will not quit until I avenge myself. Then the old man said: Let us pray, brother; and standing up, he said: O God, we no longer need you to take care of us since we now avenge ourselves. Hearing these words, the brother fell at the feet of the old man and said: I am not going to fight with my brother any more. Forgive me, Abba.

Once two brothers went to visit an old man. It was not the old man's habit, however, to eat every day. When he saw the brothers, he welcomed them with joy, and said: Fasting has its own reward, but if you eat for the sake of love you satisfy two commandments, for you give up your own will and also fulfill the commandment to refresh others.

Abba Nisteros the Great was walking through the desert with a brother, and seeing a dragon, they ran away. Then the brother said to him: Are you afraid too, Father? The old man replied: I was not afraid, my son, but it was good for me to run away from the dragon; otherwise, I would not have escaped from the spirit of vainglory.

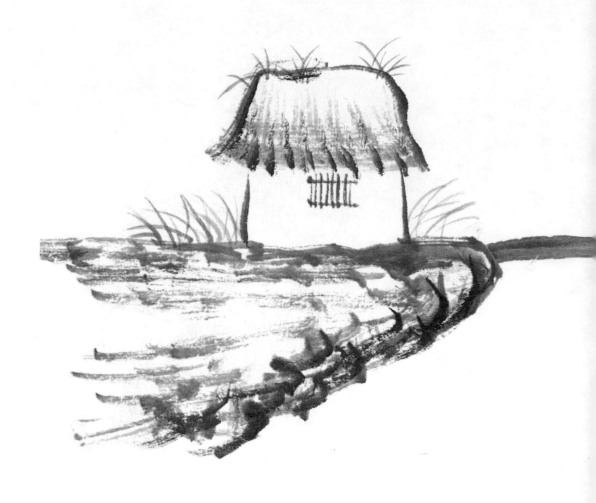

It was said about an old man that he endured seventy weeks of fasting, eating only once a week. He asked God about certain words in the Holy Scripture, but God did not answer him. Then he said to himself: Look, I have put in this much effort, but I haven't made any progress. So now I will go to see my brother, and ask him. And when he had gone out,

closed the door and started off, an angel of the Lord was sent to him, and said: Seventy weeks of fasting have not brought you near to God. But now that you are humbled enough to go to your brother, I have been sent to you to reveal the meaning of the words. Then the angel explained the meaning which the old man was seeking, and went away.

Abba Poemen said: Teach your mouth to speak what is in your heart.

Abba Poemen said: The nature of water is yielding, and that of a stone is hard. Yet if you hang a bottle filled with water above the stone so that the water drips drop by drop, it will wear a hole in the stone. In the same way the word of God is tender, and our heart is hard. So when people hear the word of God frequently, their hearts are opened to the fear of God.

59

Abba Elias said := Unless the mind sings with the body, the labor is in vain. And := Whoever loves tribulation will have joy and refreshment afterwards.

There was an old man who had a good disciple. One day he
was annoyed and drove the disciple out. Yet the disciple sat
down outside of the cell and wailed. When the old man
opened the door, he found him sitting there, and repented
before him, saying: You are my father, for your humility
and patience have overcome my narrow-mindedness. Come
inside! From now on, you are the old man and the father,
for sure, and I am the young one and the disciple. For your
good works have surpassed my old age.

When Abba Macarius was in Egypt, he found a
man with a mule stealing his belongings. Then,
as though he were a stranger, he helped the
robber to load the animal, and peacefully sent

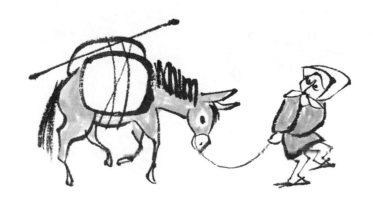

him off, saying = We have brought nothing into
the world, and we cannot take anything with
us. The Lord has given, and as he has wished, so it
has happened. Blessed be the Lord in all things.

Once some bandits came to the hermitage of an old man, and said: We have come to take away everything in your cell. And he said: Whatever you see, my sons. Then they took whatever they found in the cell and went away. But they left behind a little bag which was out of sight. But the old man picked it up, and ran after them, shouting: My sons, take this! You forgot it! They were indeed amazed by the endurance of the old man, and brought everything back into the cell. And all of them repented and said to each other: He really is a man of God.

The devil appeared to a brother, in the disguise of an angel of light, and said to him: I am the angel Gabriel and I have been sent to you. However, the brother said to him: See if you are not being sent to someone else. I certainly do not deserve to have an angel sent to me. Immediately, the devil disappeared.

A brother said to an old man: There are two brothers. One of them stays in his cell quietly, fasting for six days at a time, and imposing on himself a good deal of discipline, and the other serves the sick. Which one of

them is more acceptable to God? The old man replied: Even if the brother who fasts six days were to hang himself by the nose, he could not equal the one who serves the sick.

Abba Xanthias said: A dog is better than I am because it also has love, but it does not pass judgment.

A philosopher asked Saint Anthony: Father, how can you be enthusiastic when the comfort of books has been taken away from you? He replied: My book, O Philosopher, is the nature of created things, and whenever I want to read the word of God, it is usually right in front of me.

There were two old men who had lived together for many
years, and they never quarreled. Now one of them said:
Let us try to quarrel once just like other people do. And
the other replied: I don't know how a quarrel happens.
Then the first said: Look, I put a brick between us, and
I say, This is mine, and you say, No, it's mine, and after
that a quarrel begins. So they placed a brick between
them, and one of them said: This is mine, and the other
said: No, it's mine. And he replied: Indeed, it's all
yours, so take it away with you! And they went
away unable to fight with each other.

One old man went to visit another. As they were talking, one of them said = I am dead to this world. The other man said to him = Do not be so sure about yourself until you are really dead, for you may say that you are dead, yet Satan is not dead.

A leader of a community asked Abba Poemen: How
can I gain the fear of God? Abba Poemen replied:
How indeed can we gain the fear of God when we
have bellies full of cheese and jars of salted fish?

A noble man whom nobody knew came to Scetis carrying gold with him, and asked the priest of the desert to distribute it to the brothers. The priest said to him: The brothers do not need it. But he was very insistent and was not satisfied, so he put the whole sum in a basket at the entrance of the church. And the priest said: Whoever needs it may take some. But nobody touched it or even looked at it. Then the old man said: God has accepted your offering. Go, and give it to the poor. And the man went away greatly benefited.

Abba Sarmatas said: I prefer a person who has sinned if he knows that he sinned and has repented, over a person who has not sinned and considers himself to be righteous.

Abba Doulas, the disciple of Abba Bessarion, said:
When we were walking along the sea one day, I was
thirsty, so I said to Abba Bessarion, Abba, I am
very thirsty. Then the old man prayed, and said to me,
Drink from the sea. The water was sweet when I

drank it. And I poured it into a flask, so that I would not be thirsty later. Seeing this, the old man asked me, Why are you doing that? I answered, Excuse me, but it's so that I won't be thirsty later on. Then the old man said, God is here, and God is everywhere.

One day, Theophilus of holy memory, the bishop of Alexandria, came to Scetis. And the brothers who gathered said to Abba Pambo: Say a word to the bishop so that his soul may be benefited here. The old man replied: If he is not inspired by my silence, he will not be inspired by my words either.

Abba Poemen said: If a monk overcomes two things, he can be free from this world. And a brother asked: What are they? He replied: Bodily ease and vain-glory.

A brother came to Abba Poemen and said: Abba, a variety of thoughts are coming into my mind and I am in danger. The old man took him out in the air and said: Open your robe and take hold of the wind. And he answered: No, I cannot do it. The old man said: If you cannot do it, neither can you prevent those thoughts from coming in. But what you should do is to stand firm against them.

There was a man in Egypt whose son was paralyzed,
and he brought him to the cell of blessed Macarius,
and left him crying at the door, and went away.
Then the old man looked around, and saw the boy crying, and said to him: Who brought you here? And
he said: My father abandoned me here and left.
And the old man said: Stand up and go get him!
The boy was healed at once, and went to find
his father, and thus they went home together.

Once some people came to an old man in Thebaid, bring-
ing a person possessed by a demon, hoping that he might
be cured by the old man. Being asked persistently for
quite some time, the old man finally said to the demon:
Go out of God's creation. And the demon replied: I will
go out, but let me ask you just one thing. Tell me, who

are the goats and who are the sheep? Then the old
man said: A goat is someone such as I am, but as
for the sheep, well, only God knows. Hearing this
the demon cried out in a loud voice: Look, because
of your humility I am going out! And he went away
that very moment.

Abba Isidore of Pelusia said: Living without speaking is better than speaking without living. For a person who lives rightly helps us by silence, while one who talks too much merely annoys us. If, however, words and life go hand in hand, it is the perfection of all philosophy.

Abba Poemen said: There is one sort of person who seems to be silent, but inwardly criticizes other people. Such a person is really talking all the time. Another may talk from morning till night, but says only what is meaningful, and so keeps silence.

Amma Syncletica said: It is good not to get angry. But if it should happen, do not allow your day to go by affected by it. For it is said: Do not let the sun go down. Otherwise, the rest of your life may be affected by it. Why hate a person who hurts you, for it is not that person who is injust, but the devil. Hate the sickness, but not the sick person.

Abba Joseph asked Abba Poemen: How should we fast? And Abba Poemen said: I myself think it's good to eat every day, a little at a time, so as not to get full. Abba Joseph said: Well, when you were young, didn't you used to fast for two days at a time? And the old man said: Believe me, indeed I did, for three days, and even a week. But the great elders tried all of this, and found that it is good to eat every day, a little less each time. In this way, they showed us the royal highway, for it is light and easy.

One day, Abba Isaac the Theban went to a monastic community and he saw a brother doing wrong, and he condemned him. As he returned to the desert, an angel of the Lord came and stood in front of the door of his cell and said: I won't let you in. He asked: What's the matter? And the angel replied: God has sent me to ask you where he should cast the sinner on whom you passed judgment. Immediately he repented and said: I was wrong. Forgive me. And the angel said: Get up, God has forgiven you. In the future be sure not to judge someone before God passes judgment.

As he was dying, Abba Benjamin taught his sons this: Do this, and you'll be saved: Rejoice always, pray constantly, and in all circumstances give thanks.

Abba Or said: Either flee from people,
or laugh at the world and the people in it,
and make a fool of yourself in many things.

Abba Lot went to see Abba Joseph and said: Abba, as much as I am able I practice a small rule, a little fasting, some prayer and meditation, and remain quiet, and as much as possible I keep my thoughts clean. What else should I do? Then the old man stood up and stretched out his hands toward heaven, and his fingers became like ten torches of flame. And he said: If you wish, you can become all flame.

90

$\mathcal{A}$mma Sarah said: If I pray to God that all people might be inspired because of me, I would find myself repenting at the door of every house. I would rather pray that my heart be pure toward everybody.

Abba Nilus said: Whatever you do in revenge against your brother who has hurt you will appear all at once in your heart at the time of prayer.

The old men used to say: When we are tested, we are more humbled, for God knows our weakness and protects us. Yet when we boast, God takes his protection away from us. Then we are really lost.

Amma Theodora said: A teacher ought to be a stranger to love of domination, and a foreigner to vainglory, far from arrogance, neither deceived by flattery, nor blinded by gifts, nor a slave to the stomach, nor held back by anger, but rather should be patient, kind, and as far as possible humble. He ought to be self-disciplined, tolerant, diligent, and a lover of souls.

A brother asked an old man: What is humility? And the old man said: To do good to those who hurt you. The brother said: If you cannot go that far, what should you do? The old man replied: Get away from them and keep your mouth shut.

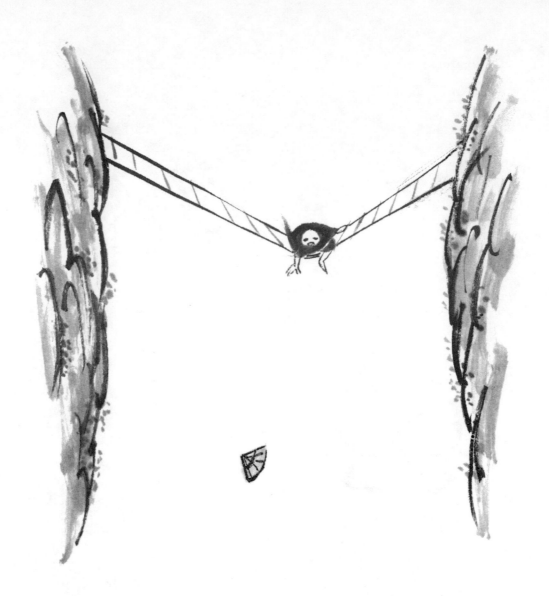

Abba Euprepios said: Bodily things consist of matter. The person who loves worldly things loves stumbling blocks. When we lose something, therefore, we should accept it with joy and thanks, as we have been relieved from care.

Abba Sisoes the Theban said to his disciple: Tell me what you see in me and in turn I will tell you what I see in you. His disciple said to him: You are good in soul, but a little harsh. The old man said to him: You are good but your soul is not tough.

Isidore of Pelusia said: Prize virtues, and do not care for worldly prosperity. For the former are certainly immortal, but the latter is so easily extinguished.

98

An old man said: Do not despise your neighbor, for you do not know whether the spirit of God is in you or in him. Well, I tell you, the one who serves you is your neighbor.

Abba Epiphanus said: God sells righteousness very cheap to those who are eager to buy: namely, for a little piece of bread, worthless clothes, a cup of cold water and one coin.

Abba Nilus said: Do not want things to turn out as they seem best to you, but as God pleases. Then you will be free of confusion and thankful in your prayer.

The brothers asked Abba Agathon: Father, which of
the virtues of our way of life demands the greatest
effort? He said to them: Forgive me, but there is
no effort comparable to prayer to God. In fact, whenever you want to pray, hostile demons try to interrupt
you. Of course they know that nothing but prayer to
God entangles them. Certainly when you undertake
any other good work, and persevere in it, you obtain
rest. But prayer is a battle all the way to the last breath.

They asked Abba Macarius: How should we pray? The old man answered: A long speech is not necessary, but instead stretch out your hands and say, Lord, as you wish and as you know, have mercy. Yet if you feel a conflict is breaking out, you have to say, Lord, help! He knows what is good for us and treats us mercifully.

A brother asked Abba Matoes: What shall I do? My tongue causes me trouble and whenever I am among people, I cannot control it and I condemn them in all their good deeds and contradict them. What, therefore, shall I do? The old man answered him: If you cannot control yourself, go away from people and live alone. For this is a weakness - Those who live together with others ought not to be square, but round, in

order to turn toward all. Further, the old man said: I live alone not because of my virtue, but rather because of my weakness. You see, those who live among people are the strong ones.

Abba James said: We do not want words alone, for there are too many words among people today. What we need is action, for that is what we are looking for, not words which do not bear fruit.

MEDITERRANEAN SEA
JERUSALEM
ALEXANDRIA
GAZA
NITRIA
SCETIS
CAIRO
LIBYAN DESERT
MT. SINAI
MT. ST. ANTHONY
EGYPT
ARABIAN DESERT
RED SEA
THEBAID
TABENNISI
THEBES